SOME DEVONIAN ITEMS

A SERIES OF MISCELLANEOUS NOTICES OF DEEDS, WILLS AND KINDRED DOCUMENTS RELATING TO DEVONSHIRE.

—

By

R. N. WORTH, F.G.S.

—

Copyright © 2018 Read Books Ltd.
This book is copyright and may not be
reproduced or copied in any way without
the express permission of the publisher in writing

British Library Cataloguing-in-Publication Data
A catalogue record for this book is available from
the British Library

SOME DEVONIAN ITEMS.

BY R. N. WORTH, F.G.S.

(Read at Ashburton, July, 1896.)

[*Reprinted from the Transactions of the Devonshire Association for the Advancement of Science, Literature, and Art.* 1896.—xxviii. pp. 323-337.]

I HAVE brought together in this paper a series of miscellaneous notices of deeds and wills and kindred documents relating to Devonshire, which have not yet found their way into print. With two exceptions they chiefly relate to the vicinity of Ashburton, Widdecombe, and Buckfastleigh, and will, I hope, be found of service by those who are interested in the local history. The exceptions are rather important—at least in one instance. I have been much indebted to Mr. W. H. Prance, of Plymouth, for a copy of the will of that notable Totnes worthy in his later life, Dr. Burthogg, who belonged, however, to the neighbourhood of Plymouth, where he had property. It was in connection with that property that the will was preserved. The other is a copy of the will of John Ilcombe, one of the most prominent merchants and corporators of Plymouth in the sixteenth century. For this I am indebted to the kindness of the Rev. J. Hall Parlby, of Manadon, among whose family papers it was found. The remaining notices generally are taken from a MS. collection in the Plymouth Proprietary Library. I give, in the first place, the two wills mentioned above in order of date:

"In the name of God Amen the xijth daie of Januarie in the xxj yere of the raigne of o^r sou'aigne Lady Elizabeth by the grace of God Queene of England Fraunce and Ireland Defend^r of the faieth &c I John Ilcomb thelder of Plymoth in the County of Devon m̃chaunte being of p̃fecte memorie, revoking all former Wills and testamets legacie and Legacies by me heoretofore at any tyme made willed named or bequeathed, do make this my last will and testament in manner and foarme following First and principally I bequeth my soule to almighty God, and my body to the earth. Item I geave and bequeth to the poore peeple of the

Towne of Plymouth where neade is xl^s in money and to the Mawlen house there x^s and to the almes house there ten shillings. Item I geeve and bequeth and assigne vnto Phe Yarde my son in lawe the lease of the Vicaridge of Plymouth and all my right title estate and terme of yeres of and in the same to have and to holde to hym and to his assignes for and during all such time and terme of yeres as I have to come of and in the same at the tyme of my deceasse. Item I geeve and bequeth to Joane Yarde my daughter my best salte of silver gilte wth the cover. I geeve and bequeth to everie of the said Philip Yards childerne xl^s of Lawfull money of England and to everie of them two silver spones. Item I geeve and bequeth to Alice pirry my daughter my best standing Cupp of Silver wth the cover of the same, and to everie of her Childerne xl^s of Lawfull money of England and to everie of them ij silver spones. Item I geeve and bequeth to Margerie Yarde the daughter of Phillip Yarde one of my Silver Gobletts gilte and my lesste sylver salte gilt Item I geeve and bequeth to Gartright Yarde the daughter of the said Phe Yarde one of my Gobletts of Silver pcell gilte. Item I geeve and bequeth to Elizabeth Corbyn my daughter my best gilt Goblett of silver wth his cover and twenty pounds of lawfull money of England. Item if it happen that my Shipp named the mynyon be, at the tyme of my deceasse abroade from home in any marchaunt Viadge then I geeve and bequeth the money dewe for the fraight of the said Shippe for the said Viadge unto Phillipp Yarde and William Pirrie my sonnes in law, to be equally devided betwene them and if the said Shipp be abroade from home in any fishinge Viadge or otherwise for p^{ts} then I geeve and bequeth all such p^{te} as appertayneth to the said Shipp for the said Viadge to the said Phillipp Yarde and Willia Pirrie to be equally devided betwixt them And if it happen the said Shippe to be at home at the tyme of my deceasse then my mynde and will is that the same Shippe wth her furnyture and apparell be indifferently preised, and being so preised I geeve and bequeth one hundred pounds of Lawfull money of England pcell of the money that the said Shipp is preised in, to the said Phillipp Yarde and William Pirrie to [be] equally devided betwixt them. Item I geeve and bequeth my house wherein I now dwelle to Christyan my wief, to have holde occupie and enioy the same to her and to her assignes duringe her naturall lief Also I geeve and bequeth to my said wief eight pounds of lawfull money of England of annuytie yerelie to be paid her out of my lands and tenements during her naturall lief and for not-payment thereof, my said lands and tenements to be strayned therefore by my said wief or one that she shall appoynt Item I geeve and bequeth to my said wief two fether bedds pfourmed freely and the rest of ij bedsteads during her lief Item I will devise and bequeth to John Ilcomb my sone and heire appareant all my messuadgs lands tenements rents revertions services and hereditaments whatsoever wth theire appurtenncs sett lying and being in Plymouth and els wheresoever in the Counties of Devon and Cornewall. To have hold and enioy the said messuadgs Lands tenements and other the premisses wth theire apptencs to the said John Ilecombe my sonne and to the heires of his body lawfully begotten and to be begotten, Vntell such tyme as the said John Ilecombe my sonne or any of the heires of his body lawfully begotten or to be begoten do make, knowledg pcure suffer or assent to be don had or made by fyne Feoffment recoverie wth voucher or vouchers or by anie other waies or meanes, any acte or acts whatsoever wher by the estate tayle or estate in fee symple here in this my present testament lymited and appoynted to the said John Ilecombe and to any other pson or psons hereafter named or to any of them shall or may be discontinued altered changed or debarred, or whereby the said messuadgs lands tenements hereditaments and other the premissis wth their appurtenncs or any pte thereof, or any estate or estats of and in the same shall or may be transferred and convayed to the hands and possession of any other pson or psons in any other sorte then tenant in tayle may doe by the Statute made in the xxxij^{th} yere of the raigne of Kynge henrie the eight entituled An Act that Lessees shall enioy their fermes against the teññte in tayle or in the right of theire wieves or Churches &c And for default of issue of the body of the said John Ilecombe my sonne Lawfully begotten or to be begoten Or if the said estate tayle shal bee sooner ended determyned or avoyded for or by reason of any cause matter or thinge before mentioned or by any other wayes, meanes or cause whatsoever Then the said messuadgs Lands tenements and other the premisses wth their appurtenncs to remayne come and be to Phillip Yarde and Johan his wief my daughter and to William Pirrie and Alice his wief my other daughter and to the heires of the bodies of the said Johan and Alice my daughter lawfully begotten and to be begoten And for default of such issue, the remaynder thereof to the right heires of me the said Ilecombe theire heires and assignes for ever To be holden of the chiefe Lords of the fee of the premises by the rents and services thereof done and of right accustomed The residue of all my goods not geeven nor bequethed both moveable and vnmoveable I geve and bequeth to Phillip Yarde my sonne in lawe whom I doe ordayne and make my sole executor of this my last will and testament and I do appoynte Mr. Nycholas Slannynge and Mr. John Amydes esquiers to be my overseers of this my last will and testament to whom I geeve for theire paynes xl^{s} a peece. Witnesses to this my testament John dyer and Edwarde Marshe of the County of Exeter."

"In the name of God Amen I Richard Burthogge late of the Town of Totnes in the County of Devon Esquire being weak in Body but strong in mind and memory do make this my last Will and Testament in manner and form following Imprimis I do commend my spirit unto God as to a faithful Creator in a firm belief of the merit and intercession of Jesus Christ my Gracious Redeemer and for my Body I bequeath it to the Earth to be rendered thereunto by a decent Burial according to the discretion of my Executrixes hereafter named and for the testamentary Estate which it hath pleased God in his great goodness to favor me with I dispose thereof in manner and form following First I give and bequeath unto Honor Burthogge my Wife the picture of her Uncle with the case and stone belonging to it Item I give and bequeath to my said Wife all the plate she had before Marriage, her China Bason, and the Bed in the Hall Chamber performed Item. I give and bequeath to my said Wife a diamond Ring which I presented to her when I courted her and do now confirm unto her Item I give and bequeath unto my said Wife the sum of Ten pounds of lawful money of England Item. I give and bequeath unto Sr Richard Gipps the sum of Thirty shillings to buy him a Mourning Ring Item I give and bequeath to Mr Richard Gipps Son of the said Sr Richard Gipps Thirty shillings to buy him a Mourning Ring Item I give and bequeath unto Sr John Elwill Forty shillings to buy him a Mourning Ring Item I give and bequeath to Edward Stephens of Lygrove in the County of Gloster Esqr Thirty shillings to buy him a Mourning Ring Item. I give and bequeath unto the said Edward Stephens the whole and sole benefit and advantage of any two lives nominated by him and to be put in on that Messuage and Tenement situate lying and being in the Parish of Aishbrenton als Ashprington under the ancient and accustomed rents and services and which is now in the possession of Richard Fosse in reversion of the present Estate of the said Richard Fosse of and in the same Item I give and bequeath unto Philip Mayow of Bray Esqr Thirty shillings to buy him a Mourning Ring Item. I give and bequeath unto Sarah Stephens my Daughter Wife of the said Edward Stephens the sum of Threescore pounds of lawfull money of England in satisfaction of the like sum lent by me out of her money to my Cosen Christopher Ceely tho' she hath released me of it Item I further give and bequeath to my said Daughter Sarah Stephens Forty pounds of like lawful money as a token of my particular affection to her item I give and bequeath to Richard Babbage the son of my Daughter Ann Babbage deceased a Hundred pounds of like lawful money to bind him out an Apprentice and Fifty pounds more of like lawful money to set up with all at the end of his Apprenticeship Item my Will is and accordingly I do charge and oblige my Executrixes their $Exec^{rs}$ and Adm^{rs} that before and till the said Richard Babbage shall be bound out an Apprentice they one or some of them do pay or cause to be paid to the said Richard Babbage or to his use Nine pounds yearly by even and quarterly payments at the most usual days of payment Item I give and bequeath to my Sister Mrs Elizabeth Harwood of Foy Forty pounds of like lawful money Item I give and bequeath unto Madamosel Margaret de Malromes Fifty pounds of like lawful money in consideration of her great care and attendance of me in my great sickness at Bowden and in full recompence of any money whatsoever that hath been due to her for her service with me Item I give and bequeath unto Mrs Alice Ceely Widow Ten pounds of lawful money of England Item I give and bequeath unto Mr Arch Deacon Burscough Forty shillings to buy him a Mourning Ring Item I give and bequeath unto Mr Edmund Elys Forty shillings to buy him a Mourning Ring Item I give and bequeath unto Mr Mullins Forty shillings to buy him a Mourning Ring Item I give and bequeath unto Mr Thomas Hancock the elder Forty shillings to buy him a Mourning Ring Item I give and bequeath unto Mr Theophilus Tinckham Forty shillings to buy him a Mourning Ring Item I give and bequeath unto Mr John Deeble Thirty shillings to buy him a Mourning Ring Item I give and bequeath unto Mr William Bowden Thirty shillings to buy him a Mourning Ring Item I give and bequeath unto Mrs Mary Coode Thirty shillings to buy her a Mourning Ring Item I give and bequeath unto Thomas Hancock my Servant Forty shillings to buy him a Mourning Ring Item I give and bequeath unto Mrs Galpin, Widow, Forty shillings to buy her a Mourning Ring Item I give and bequeath unto Mr James Rowe and to Elizabeth his Wife Forty shillings to each of them to buy them Mourning Rings Item I give unto Mary Hooper my Servant Forty shillings Item I give unto Mrs Tottle twenty shillings Item I give and devise all my Messuages lands tenements and hereditaments whatsoever with their appurts lying and being within the Town and parish of Plymouth and within the Town and parish of Modbury and also within the parish of Ashbrenton also Ashprington in the County of Devon and likewise my fee Farm rent issuing and growing due out of the Manor of Ashbrenton also Ashprington aforesaid unto my Daughter Sarah Stephens aforesaid and to the first son of her Body lawfully begotten or to be begotten and to the heirs Males of the Body of such first Son lawfully begotten or to be begotten and for want of such issue then to the second third fourth fifth sixth seventh eighth ninth tenth and every other Son or Sons of the said Sarah Stephens and every of their priority of birth and seniority of age and for default of such issue then I give and devise all and every th' aforesaid messuages lands tenements hereditaments and fee farm rent to my daughter Mary Mayow the Wife of Philip Mayow aforesaid and to the first Son of her Body lawfully begotten or to be begotten and to the heirs males of the Body of such first Son and for want of such issue then to the second third fourth fifth sixth seventh eighth ninth tenth and to every other Son and Sons of the said Mary Mayow born of her Body as aforesaid and to the heirs Males of the Body of all and every such Son and Sons as aforesaid wherein the Owner and heirs of his Body is and are always to be preferred and to take before the Younger and the heirs Males of his Body according to their and every of their priority of birth and seniority of age and for want of such issue then to Richard Babbage aforesaid on this Condition and not otherwise that he the said Richard Babbage do leave and reject the name of Babbage and instead thereof to take and bear the name of Burthogge for his surname and to the heirs Males of his Body if they take and bear the name of Burthogge and not otherwise and for default of such issue Male or if the said Richard Babbage or any of his said heirs refuse or neglect to take the name of Burthogge as aforesaid then to the issue male of the said Sarah Stephens and to the heirs of the Body and Bodies of such issue female and for default of such issue to the issue Female of the said Mary Mayow and to the heirs of the Body and Bodies of such issue female and in defect of such issue to my right heirs for ever Provided always that if the aforesaid Honor Burthogge my Wife do prove to be now with child (as she says she is) and the said Child shall be a male child then I give and devise all my messuages lands tenements and hereditaments and fee farm rent aforesaid unto such Male child and his heirs for ever but if the same child shall be a Female child then I give and devise only my aforesaid messuages lands tenements and hereditaments that are lying and being in the Town and parish of Modbury aforesaid unto such issue female and her heirs for ever Item I give and bequeath unto John Shapleigh of New Court in the County of Devon aforesaid Esquire Forty shillings to buy him a Mourning ring in remembrance of the great respect I had for his Father and kindness for him Item I do hereby nominate ordain and appoint my Trustee and well beloved Friend Servinton Savery of Shilstone in the County of Devon Esquire Mr Christopher Farewell of Totnes aforesaid Merchant and Mr John Trehawke of Liskeard in the County of Cornwall Mercer my Overseers in trust to advise and assist my said daughter Sarah Stephens and Mary Mayow in ordering and disposing of the Estate hereby given to them Item I give and bequeath to my said Overseers in trust Forty shillings to each of them to buy them Mourning Rings Item I will that all these debts and duties I owe in right or conscience to any manner of person or persons whatsoever shall be well and truly contented and paid or ordained to be paid by my Executrix named within convenient time after my decease Item All the rest of my Goods and Chattels real and personal not hereinbefore given and bequeathed I give and bequeath unto my said two Daughters Sarah Stephens and Mary Mayow whom I make and ordain the whole and sole Executrixes of this my last Will and Testam^t annulling and making void all Wills and Testaments whatsoever by me formerly made and this I do publish and declare to be my last Will and Testament subscribed with my name and sealed with my Seal this five and twentyeth day of March in the Year our Lord God according to the Computation of the Church of England One thousand seven hundred and five

"Signed sealed published and declared to be the last Will and Testament of the above named Richard Burthogge Esqre in the presence of

Richard Burthogge

(SEAL.)

"John Olver
Stephen Sleep
Tristrum Hicks
Jane Short"

John Mugge grants a piece of land which he had of the gift of Wm. Corbin, to Henry Baillif. Witnesses—John of Kylloby, John of Boymla, Peter of Woddeton, Wm. Tyrtape, Stephen Wymund. Dated Legh Buff, 13 Edward II.

John ffalewylle and Walter Scobetorr grant to John Mugge, of Scoryaton, all the lands at Bukfastlegh and elsewhere in Devon, which they had of his gift and feoffment, after his death to go to his son Thomas, and Stephen his brother, in reversion, failing heir to Thomas. Stephen to have 10s. a year out of Kanelaton. Witnesses—John Benyle, Wm. Gybbe, John Boynyle, Giles Mugge, John Mugge, jun. Dated at Scobetorre, Scoryaton, Wednesday after St. Martin, 5 Henry IV.

William Martyn, clerk, son of Clarice, late wife of Richard Martyn, of Bokfastlegh, gent., claims to Wm. Cola, of Plymouth, his right to a meadow in Buckfastleigh, between the land of Geoffrey, Virtia east, the King's way south, a water called M'lnor north. Dated at Plymouth, Dec., 36 Edward III. Witnesses—Roger Boswynes, Wm. Orchet, John Boswynes, Richard Ferrers, John Trenyhaux.

Grant by Wm. Woode, of Ugborough, and Nycholl, his wife, to Edward Grey, husbandman, Joan, his wife, and John their son, their moiety of a tenement in Buckfastlegh, in which John Colman the elder, Agnes his wife, and John Colman the younger are also interested. 1st Sep., 10 Elizabeth.

Presentation by Richard Cabell to the vicarage of Buckfastleigh, vacant by the death of John Tolbeare, of John Courtice, clerk, 1642.

"In the name of god Amen the xvth daye of ffebruary yn the yere of o^r lord Jh̅us x̃pus m̊ ccccc xxxviijth I WILLIAM PHYLYPPE of bookefastligh perfytt of mynde and hole of Remembraunce make my testamente declarying my last wylle yn thys man̅ß ffolowyng FFURSTE I bequeth my sowle vnto Almyghthy god AND my body to holy erth to be buryed yn the Churche yerde of the trynyte of Bookefasteligh Itn y bequeth to the syx p'ncypalle stowrs of the churche of the same Bookefasteligh equally to be payd ij^s & to the trynyte high crosse saynt Kateryne o^r lady the grome S^{tn} & and the bells sto^r & to eury of them iiij^d. ITM to Syr herry macy viij^d Itn to my brother Nycolas x^s and the xviij^{ti} pte of my týnworke callyd WYTTHYNG I geve to my Brother Rycharde and yn mony x^s ITN to my Syster Rycharde xl^s Itn y geve vnto my fadre Williā phylyppe the syxt parte of my tynworke callyd Smalle mony ITN to my brother John phylyppe the xijth parte of the Same worke callyd Smalle mony Itn to my brother Rycharde the syxt pte of the same worke The lyvery thereof Rez yn the hands of John Halle : Itn to the vycar of Bookefasteligh for tythys forgoten, vj^d ITN y geve to my Brother Rycharde phylyppe my hole ryght tytle and ynterest w^t all com̅odyts and pfets that y have and herafter thys ough to have yn hullond w^t yn button yn the pyshe of Bookefasteligh whyche now holdyth John Clyffe and thereof hath a state for trme of hys owne lyffe and Chrystyane hys wyffe after whose deptyng yn and of the same hullonde I have Ren̅ßcyone for ffoorescore yere to me and my assignys as mo^r at large apperyth by the dede thereof made by danyell mugge esquyer & lord thereof whos date ys the x. day of octobre yn the xxixth yere of the Raygne of o^r Soverent lord kyng henry the viijth THE Resydewe of all my goods I geve and bequeth to John and Rycharde my brothers whom I make my hole executors to do therew^t what shalle plese thẽ best herevnto sevyth wytnys herry macy, william phylyppe, Thom̅s M'tyn, and other desyred & requyred, &c."

Inquisition held at Plympton by John Rattenbury, escheator, January 23rd, 3 James I., on the death of William Phillipp. Jury found that he died seized of one toft, three acres of land, one acre of meadow, six acres of pasture, and one acre of wood in the parish of Buckfastleigh called Mirefeild, and that they were held of the King as of his manor of Buckfastleigh, part of the dissolved abbey of Buckfastleigh, by the annual rent of xij^d. That the said Phillipp died at Shereford, 12th December, 1 James I.; and that Chrstopher Phillip, his son and heir, was of full age.

Draft of an Inquisition *post-mortem* taken in an unnamed year of Henry VIII., on the death of Daniel Mugge (afterwards called Mudge) generosus. Thomas Seyntleger and others had been seized of the manor of Button, in the parish of Bukfastleghe, at Suthholle to the uses of Walter Mugge and his heirs. The said Walter Mugge, by his will made at Guldeford, Surrey, left the said manor to Joan his wife term of her life, and on her death to the said Daniel Mugge and the heirs of his body lawfully begotten. Thomas Seyntleger and all his fellow feoffees having died with the exception of Richard Hussey, the manor was vested in him until he died also, when he was succeeded in the feoffment by his grandson Thomas Hussey (son of William, son of Richard). On a certain day of February, in the 27th year of Henry VIII., Daniel Mudge, by a certain statute, became seized of the manor for himself and the heirs of his body lawfully begotten, and was so seized when he died. The heirs then were Joan Jones, widow, Anne, wife of John Aleyn, and William More generosus—the same Joan and Anne being daughters of the said Walter Mugge, and William More, kinsman and heir of Walter Undell, son of Margaret More, defunct, another daughter and heir of the said Walter Mudge. So the jury find that the aforesaid manor of Button belongs to them, and that its value, beyond reprises, was £8 11s. 4½d. a year. They also found that Daniel had no other lands or houses in Devon, and that he died at Guldeford, in the county of Surrey, on the last day of December, 33 Henry VIII. Further, that the said Joan, Anne, and Walter were of full age when the inquisition was taken; and that Isabella Mugge, widow, had been wife of the deceased.

Inquisition *post-mortem* on the death of Stephen Addam of Buckfastleigh, taken by Christopher Asmond, escheator, at Chudley, April 5, 1 James I. Had ten acres of arable, two pasture, one wood, ten rush and heath, on Warmacombe, Buckfastleigh, and the fifth part of two messuages, one garden, ten acres of arable meadow and pasture in Sulebar, Mevy, and of common pasture in waste and wood of Sulebar —the former held of Richard Cavill of his manor of Maynbowe, the latter of Barnardo howde of his manor of Grenevill. He had died on the 21st June previous, and John Addams, 26 and above, was his son and heir.

Surrender by Ann Greene, widow of John Greene, tanner, of Buckfastlegh, to Sir Richard Baker of Middle Aston, Oxon., of two closes parcel of Twyn stiles, lying between Rowdon Crosse and the Church Crosse, in the north part of Twynstiles, and a parcel of land called Revercomb. Consideration £200. 5th June, 1629.

Copy of Court Roll of Buckfast 24th Feb., 16 Charles II., Sir George Sands and Sir Robert Parkhurst, lords, transferring tenement held by Richard Chaffe, sen^r, and Richard Chaffe, ju^r, to Henry Luscombe, Susannah his wife, and Elizabeth their daughter.

William Ellacott, Nicholas Cooke, and John Warren, defendants, making answer, Jan. 20th, 1654, to a Bill of Complaint preferred by Richard Cabell, esq., complainant, say

"they do not knowe that the Complainant is debtor vnto the said Lord Protector in the bill named or that o^r late Soveraigne Lord King James was seized at all of and in the Manno^r of Buckfastleigh . . . but doe deny that the Milles called the Towne Milles . . . are or ever were parcell of or belonging vnto the said Manno^r. And these defendants do not know . . . whether the Complt have any lawfull estate at all in the said Mills. . . . And these defendts and every of them doe deny that either the Customary teñnts and occupiers of any Messuages lands or Tenements w^thin or holden of the said Manno^r or the Resiants or Inhabitants wthin the same haue by all the time whereof the memori of man is not to the contrary vsed and accustomed or of right and by custome ought to grind all their corne graine grist and mault spent and vsed in there seu? all and respective howses at the said mills or at one of them . . . or that either the said Teñnts or Resiants ought to paye any reasonable tolle for the grinding thereof at the said mille by any custome."

They deny that any of the tenants or residents have no right to resort to other mills, and that

"any owner or miller of any other mill or mills whatsoever or any of their Loader or Loaders by any custome whatsoever ought not to enter or come w^thin the p'cincts of the said Manno^r to take and fetch any Corne, graine, grist or mault of or from any the Teñnt or Teñnts of the said Mann^{rs} or of or from any other pson or psons inhabiting or residing w^thn the same, and to carry the said corne graine grist or mault to any other mill or mills whatsoever to bee there ground. And the sd defendts doe somewhat wonder and admire that the Complt should p'tend any such custome, for tht the Complt well knoweth it to bee true and these defendts are ready to prove that the Complainant being owner of other certain mills called Brooke Mills neere adioyning vnto or nor farre distant from the said Towne Mills did heretofore for a long time and before hee had any interest in the said Towne Mills vsually and constantly pvide and maintaine a horse and a Loader to fetch and carry any Corne graine grist and mault of and from the Teñnts of the said Manno^r and the Inhitants of the Towne of Buckfastleigh next adioyning

vnto the said Towne Mills and did accordingly vse to grind the
same at the said Brooke Mills and to recarry the same wthout
any lawfull interrupcon."

Moreover, had the custom alleged ever existed "the same
is nowe vtterly destroyed and antiquated by desuetude and
vsage to the contrary by all the time whereof the memory
of man is not to the contrary." The complainant had also
shown that in the seventh year of James I. the mills had
been severed from being part of the Manor, while when
his miller was presented in the Manor Court for taking
unreasonable toll, "the Complt being a Counsellor at lawe
the next Courte day after came vnto the said Courte and
then and there positively asserted and affirmed for law that
his mills were not and should not bee tyed to the Customes
of the said Manno^r nor the miller tryed in that Courte, but
if any of the teñnts had receaved wrong that way they
should seeke their remedy at the Common lawe."

So the defendants aver that Tennants Residents and
Inhabitants alike "time whereof memory of man is not
to the contrary," had used to grind at what mills they chose.

For three years past the millers of the Town Mills had
not "taken only reasonable and moderate tolls." They did
not know that the mills were sufficient for their work, but
rather "beleeve the contrary for that in Somer time these
three mills called the Town Mills have but one stream of
water and when one of them grindes the other two stand
still."

Ellacot, it is admitted, rented the Kilbury Mills, about half
a mile from the Town Mills, being not only a Miller but a
Loader. Whether, however, the defendants resided in the
manor of Buckfastleigh, or what were its precise "lymits
and p'cincts" they knew not; but they acknowledged that
they refused to grind at the Town Mills, and though they
denied persuading others so to do, yet they conceived they
might justify the doing thereof.

For three years Ellacot had fetched great part of the
grain belonging to Cooke and Waring and ground the same
at Kilbury Mills at a reasonable toll, "but howe the Complainant should hereby be vtterly disabled to paye his
p'tended yearly rent of fower pounds and one penny this
defendt William Ellacott doth not know, for that he did
heretofore hold the said Towne Mills of the Complt at the
yearly rent of fifty five pounds and would have continued to
hold the same longer at the yearly rent of ffifty pounds if

the Complt had pleased although the Teñnts and Resiants w^thin the said Manno^r did then (as formerly they had vsed) grinde their Corne, graine, grist and mault at the said Kilbury Mills and other places." Ellacott indeed had desired Cabell "to vse some meanes whereby to constraine them to grinde at the said Towne Mills if hee had any right or by any custom could do, but the Complainant himself confessed vnto this defendt that there was no such Custome whereby hee could constraine the Teñnts or others ... wherevpon the said Defendt left the said Towne Mills and took the said Kilbury Mills at wch the Complt ... is causelessly displeased wth him."

Cooke and Waring further declare that the "Kilbury Mills are very auntient mills, and beyond the memory of any man living to the contrary and in goodenesse and tatelynesses farre exceed and surpasse the said Towne Mills and driven all the Sumer wth two sufficient streames of water." At the Town Mills not only was too much toll taken, but the grain ill ground, by which their customers sustained great loss and prejudice. At Kilbury, on the contrary, the grinding was good and the toll-dish fair. Furthermore, they say that the Town Mill millers " have vsed to drawe and take vpp their mill hoope and to rid and cleare the hope of the said Mills and to take away the dunning that was included w^thin the said hoope the wch is very p'iudiciall to the party that doth grinde Corne or mault in such mill soe cleared, and next after such dunning soe vnlawfully taken awaye and before the said hoope be full againe and in soe great hoopes as these of the Town Mills are (it may be to the losse of the party next grinding of at least a peck and halfe of his Corne or rather more out of one bushell the wch is not vsed in the said Kilbury Mills."

Moreover, the grain was fetched and delivered from the Kilbury Mills "very beneficiall and a great ease to these defendts and others"; all which the miller of the Town Mills did not do. On the other hand, he had "given out in speeches" that the complainant would spend three hundred pounds to make the defendants grind at his mills. Having "a very great estate" this he might very well do; while the defendants were poor men, unable to maintain their just rights in law against him. Finally they denied "all plotting, practice, and combinacon both amongst themselves or wth any other pson or psons whatsoever for any the sinister ends in the Bill complained of or otherwise."

The answer was taken at Totnes 20th Jan., 1654, by John Brooking and others.

John Hale of Buckfastleigh, yeoman, sells to Robert Noseworthie of Manaton, yeoman, all his property in Buckfastleigh and Ashburton. 14th April, 21 (?) James I.

"From Hundred Rolls. Edward I.

"Villata de Aspton

"Vereɖcm xij jur' villate de Asp'ton vidett Willi Body Nichi Soril Hugon' Prigge Robi de la Weye Jacobi de Somerwille Ade Thomas Walti de Kyngdon Michis Fᵃnceys Rici de Horugg Rog'ri Russel Tristram Attapole and Willi de Marescal qui dicunt sup sacrm̄ suū ad illū articulū.

"de feud dni Reg' & ten' ejus qui ea modo teneant de ipŏ in capite &c.

"decūt gɖ ɖns Exon' epš tenet ɖcam villata de Asp'ton de ɖno Rege in capite & ptinet ad baroniam epi Exon' et dns ēps Exon' debet tvenvie p tota baronia duas milites cū ōmodis armis ad s'vic ɖni Reg' qū vocē ħat ad s'vici' p'dcm in exercitu p q°dragenta dies ad custū suū p p'm̄

"Item ad illū articlm qui aute allii a Rege clamant ħre &c.

"dicunt qɖ ɖns eps Eton' habet in ɖea villata assissas panis & s'visie & alias lit-tates qui ad burgū ptinent a quo tempe nesciūt.

"de om̄ib3 aliis articlis quot sunt dicunt se nihil scire In cuj' rei testim' p'dci jur' p'senti vereɖco sigilla sua appos-u'nt.

"[In dorso] Burg' de Asp'ton."

John Marshewyll, and Alice his wife, had granted their lands in Ayshberton and elsewhere in Devon, after their death, to Walter Marshewyll their son. He being dead, John Marshewyll aforesaid now grants the same to Walter Antron and Alianora his wife, who had been wife of the said Walter Marshewyll. Witnesses—Wm. Dolbeare, constable of Ayshberton, Richard Knollyng, prepositus of the burgh, John South jnr., John Benyshyll, Roger Torryng, and many others. 6th April, 38 Henry VI.

Geoffrey Cole grants Michael Wymund, of Ruthereford, six pieces of land in Ruthereford, five lying between Scoryaton and Ruthereford, the King's way between Ruthereford and Scoriaton west and Corbinsdowne east, the sixth south of the water of Ruthereford between Pycche and the way called Tortrowe in length, and the King's way between Ruthereford and Grendwille in breadth. Witnesses—John of Kylleby, Peter of Woddaton, Geoffrey Mugge, Henry Ballif, William Tyrcapel. Dated Ruthereforde, Wednesday before St. Margaret, 7 Edward III.

William Turckapel grants to his son Henry Turckapel all his lands in Toppesrewe, which Nicholas Cole had held; all his lands of Couleton and his pieces of land in Toppesrewe, which Thomas Cole had held—the last lying apparently south of the way from Forde to Rothereforde. Witness— Peter of Woddeton or Doddeton, William of Kyllebury, Geoffrey Mugge, Michael Chalveleigh, Michael Wymund. Dated at Couleton, Thursday after the Purification, 18 Edward III.

Robert Eliot, of Hosefenne, grants to Michael Eliot, son of Robert Eliot, of Hosefenne, a messuage in Colleforde. Witnesses — Peter of Boddeton, Geoffrey Mugge, John Mugge, Michael Wymund, Michael of Chaveleghe, and others. Dated Bucfastr, nativity of John the Baptist, 21 Edward III.

John of Hosefenne grants Michael of Hosefenne land in Ooulacom. Witnesses—John Mugge, Michael Wymund, Michael Mugge, Philip Srvyngham, Peter Toker. Dated Oulacom, 32 Edward III.

Walter Smale, and Alice his wife, grant Thomas Penpoll their messuage in North Tauston, Wydecomb. Witnesses— William Elyot, Thomas Appetorr, Wm. Leswill, John Rock, Robert Baker, Robert Wydecomb. Thursday before nativity of St. John Baptist, 31 Henry VI.

Grant of Wode in Wydecome by John atte Wode to Henry and Lucy Speke. Witnesses—Thomas atte Wode, John Coche, Roger Petorr, Thomas Elyott, Richard ffoxford.

Grant by Richard Hals, of Ratre, to Christian Wydecomb, widow of Roger Wydecomb, his tenement of Blakslade, in the parish of Wydecomb in the more, for eighty years in reversion, after her death, to Thomas Wydecomb, Joan his wife, and Marshall their son. 6th Aug., 35 Hen. VIII.

Edward Leyman, son and heir of John Leyman, £10 being paid, grants to Christopher Langworthy, son of John Langworthy, of Hatteshyll, all his rights in Nottejsworthye and elsewhere in Wydecombe. 9th May, 3 Edward VI.

John Peke, of Bridgwater, lets Wm. Byckfford, of Ilsington, his moiety or halfendeale of messuage in Dunston Wythecomb for 21 years. 21st Oct., 10 Elizabeth.

John Cater, of Wythecombe, husbandman, lets tenement of Woode for life to Margaret Gibbe, of Dunshe dyvoke, widow. 13th Aug., 13 Elizabeth.

Robert Hamlyn, of Widdecomb, yeoman, £18 having been paid, lets Blackyslade for life to John Serell, of Withecomb, husbandman, and Margeryte his wife. 28th Sept., 18 Elizabeth.

Christopher Cater, of Wydecome als Withicome, yeoman, sells to Richard Cabell various properties in Widdecombe, near the Hamlet of Woode, to wit—the parke, the Crosse park, Brome park, Hetheland, Raddehill, Nepehey, Blackpear, Pixypear, Benchey, Southemeade, Northmeade, Landy the Pittes, the Landy strave.

Augustene Hexte, of Wedycombe, yeoman, leases to Richard Smerdon, of Wedycombe, and Johanna his wife, the halfendeale or moytye of his lands and tenements in Nottysworthye, otherwise Nottesworthy heedde, with common of pasture on Hameldon, at all times of the year. 25 Elizabeth.

John Hext, of Kyngston Staverton, yeoman, enters into a bond to keep all the agreements he has entered into with Richard Hamlyn, 25th April, 2 Elizabeth. Hamlyn, who was of Widecombe in the Moor, had, it appears by another deed, paid £6 for a property " Sen desgut pnemen Venton."

Humfrie Addames, of Widdycombe, and Humfrie balle, of Chudleigh, sell to John Wheton and John Drew, of Alphington, all their estate in the tenement of Nottesworthye als Nottesworthey halle and Lyltarcombe. (In the tenure of Wheton and probably of Drew.) 26 Elizabeth.

Inquisition held at Dartmouth by Thomas Herle, escheator, 18th July, 23 Elizabeth, on death of Richard Pitton. Jury found that he died seized of a messuage, thirty acres of land, twenty of pasture, five of meadow, and five of rushes and heath called Pitton, in the parish of Wyddecomb; also a stamping mill called Pitton mill. That they were held of Thomas Southcott, of his manor of Southall. That the said Pitton died 10th June, 16 Elizabeth; and that his son Thomas, of South Brent—at his father's death twenty-three years and upwards—was the heir.

www.ingramcontent.com/pod-product-compliance
Lightning Source LLC
LaVergne TN
LVHW041526070426
835507LV00013B/1857